Symbols of America

U.S. CAPITOL

TABLE OF CONTENTS

A Crabtree Seedlings Book

CRABTREE
Publishing Company
www.crabtreebooks.com

School-to-Home Support for Caregivers and Teachers

This book helps children grow by letting them practice reading. Here are a few guiding questions to help the reader with building his or her comprehension skills. Possible answers appear here in red.

Before Reading:

• What do I think this book is about?
  • *I think this book is about the United States Capitol Building.*
  • *I think this book is about the history of the building of the U.S Capitol.*

• What do I want to learn about this topic?
  • *I want to learn more about other buildings in Washington, D.C.*
  • *I want to learn more about special rooms in the Capitol Building.*

During Reading:

• I wonder why...
  • *I wonder why there are so many works of art in the Capitol Building.*
  • *I wonder why the inauguration of the president and vice president takes place at the Capitol Building.*

• What have I learned so far?
  • *I have learned that Thomas Jefferson was the first president to be inaugurated at the Capitol.*
  • *I have learned that the 8 paintings in the rotunda tell the early history of America.*

After Reading:

• What details did I learn about this topic?
  • *I have learned that the Senate meets in the north wing of the Capitol Building.*
  • *I have learned that the House of Representatives meets in the south wing.*

• Read the book again and look for the vocabulary words.
  • *I see the word **rotunda** on page 9, and the word **oath** on page 14. The other glossary words are on pages 22 and 23.*

U.S. CAPITOL

The U.S. Capitol Building is a **symbol** of America.

Washington, D.C.

It is in Washington, D.C.

The Capitol Building is where Congress meets to write **laws**.

The Senate meets in the north wing. The House of Representatives meets in the south wing.

There are underground tunnels and a private subway in the Capitol Building.

The Statue of Freedom is on top of the Capitol **dome**.

The **rotunda** in the center has many works of art.

There are 100 statues, two from each state. Some of them are in the National Statuary Hall.

The largest statue is of King Kamehameha I. It was donated by Hawaii. It is 16 feet (4.8 meters) high and weighs about 15,000 pounds (6,800 kg).

Construction of the Capitol Building started in 1793.

As the country added states, the north and south ends got bigger.

The **inauguration** of the president and vice president takes place at the Capitol Building. They both say the **Oath** of Office.

Thomas Jefferson was the first president to be inaugurated at the Capitol Building.

The rotunda has 8 paintings in a circle.

They tell the story of America.

The Capitol has many important paintings. One showing the Signing of the Declaration of Independence is very famous.

Many people go to the visitor center built underground.

The Capitol Building is an important symbol of America.

Glossary

dome (dowm): A rounded roof of a building

inauguration (uh-naagyr-AY-shn): A ceremony that marks the beginning of something

laws (laaz): Rules created by a government

oath (oth): A formal promise

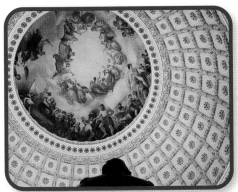

rotunda (row-TUHN-duh): A round building or room

symbol (SIM-bl): A thing that represents something else

Index

About the Author

Christina Earley lives in sunny South Florida with her husband and son. She enjoys traveling around the United States and learning about different historical places. Her hobbies include hiking, yoga, and baking.

CRABTREE
Publishing Company

Written by: Christina Earley
Designed by: Kathy Walsh
Proofreader: Petrice Custance

Photographs: Shutterstock: cover: ©Keith Lamond; ©MT511, ©dz; Title Pg: ©MT511, ©dz; Pg 4-21 ©MT511; Pg 3 & 23: ©Maria_Ermolenko; Pg 5, 22: ©Rob Crandall; Pg 6: ©njene; Pg 7: ©Rolf_52; Pg 8, 22: ©Tupungato; Pg 8: ©Jakub Zajic; Pg 9, 23: ©James Kirkikis; Pg 10: © Florin Cnejevici; Pg 11: ©Daniel M. Silva; Pg 13: ©Library of Congress; Pg 14, 22, 23: ©Joseph Sohm; Pg 15: ©BrianPIrwin; Pg 16: ©Jakub Zajic; Pg 18: © Bob Pool; Pg 19: @Wiki; Pg 20: ©Joseph Sohm; Pg 21: ©Dan Thornberg

Library and Archives Canada
Cataloguing in Publication
CIP available at Library and Archives Canada

Library of Congress Cataloging-in-Publication Data
CIP available at Library of Congress

Crabtree Publishing Company

www.crabtreebooks.com   1-800-387-7650

Printed in the U.S.A./072022/CG20220201

Published in the United States
Crabtree Publishing
347 Fifth Avenue, Suite 1402-145
New York, NY, 10016

Published in Canada
Crabtree Publishing
616 Welland Ave.
St. Catharines, Ontario L2M 5V6